inside
EMERGENCY
vehicles

By Steve Parker
Illustrated by Alex Pang

Miles
Kelly

First published in 2010 by Miles Kelly Publishing Ltd
Harding's Barn, Bardfield End Green, Thaxted, Essex, CM6 3PX, UK

Copyright © Miles Kelly Publishing Ltd 2010

This edition printed in 2012

10 9 8 7 6 5 4 3 2 1

Publishing Director: *Belinda Gallagher*
Creative Director: *Jo Cowan*
Design Concept: *Simon Lee*
Volume Design: *Rocket Design*
Cover Designer: *Simon Lee*
Indexer: *Gill Lee*
Production Manager: *Elizabeth Collins*
Reprographics: *Stephan Davis, Thom Allaway*
Consultants: *John and Sue Becklake*
Edition Editor: *Amanda Askew*

ISBN 978-1-84810-839-4

Printed in China

British Library Cataloguing-in-Publication Data
A catalogue record for this book is available from the British Library

Every effort has been made to acknowledge the source and copyright
holder of each picture. Miles Kelly Publishing apologises for any
unintentional errors or omissions.

MADE WITH PAPER FROM
A SUSTAINABLE FOREST

ACKNOWLEDGEMENTS

All panel artworks by Rocket Design
The publishers would like to thank the following sources
for the use of their photographs:
Alamy: 6(t) Interfoto; 13 Tom Wood; 14 Justin Kase z07z;
18 David Gowans
Corbis: 11 Narendra Shrestha/epa
Fotolia: 36 Gorran Haven
Getty Images: 17 John Li/Stringer; 23 Shaun Curry/
Stringer
Rex Features: 6(b) Sipa Press; 26 Sipa Press; 29 Phil
Yeomans; 32 Kenneth Ferguson
Shutterstock: COVER James Steidl, Eric Gevaert; 7(c) Jerry
Sharp; 7(b/r) corepics; 8 Colin Hutchings; 21 MISHELLA;
25 Bram van Borekhoven; 30 Eric Gevaert; 35 Jorg
Hackemann
All other photographs are from Miles Kelly Archives

WWW.FACTSFORPROJECTS.COM

Each top right-hand page directs
you to the Internet to help you
find out more. You can log on
to **www.factsforprojects.com**
to find free pictures, additional
information, videos, fun activities
and further web links. These
are for your own personal use
and should not be copied or
distributed for any commercial
or profit-related purpose.

If you do decide to use the
Internet with your book, here's a
list of what you'll need:
• A PC with Microsoft® Windows®
  XP or later versions, or a
  Macintosh with OS X or later,
  and 512Mb RAM

• A browser such as Microsoft®
  Internet Explorer 9, Firefox 4.X
  or Safari 5.X
• Connection to the Internet.
  Broadband connection
  recommended.
• An account with an Internet
  Service Provider (ISP)
• A sound card for listening to
  sound files

Links won't work?
www.factsforprojects.com is
regularly checked to make sure
the links provide you with lots
of information. Sometimes you
may receive a message saying
that a site is unavailable. If this
happens, just try again later.

Stay safe!
When using the Internet, make
sure you follow these guidelines:
• Ask a parent's or a guardian's
  permission before you log on.
• Never give out your personal
  details, such as your name,
  address or email.
• If a site asks you to log in or
  register by typing your name
  or email address, speak to your
  parent or guardian first.
• If you do receive an email from
  someone you don't know, tell
  an adult and do not reply to the
  message.
• Never arrange to meet anyone
  you have talked to on the
  Internet.

Miles Kelly Publishing is not
responsible for the accuracy or
suitability of the information on
any website other than its own.
We recommend that children are
supervised while on the Internet
and that they do not use Internet
chat rooms.

www.mileskelly.net
info@mileskelly.net

CONTENTS

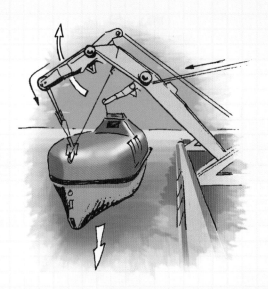

INTRODUCTION

Long ago, there were no emergency services – no paramedics, firefighters or lifeboat crews. People put out their own fires, and risked their lives in doing so. Crime was rife as there was no organized police force, and without ambulances people often died before reaching hospital. Even when emergency services were available, there was no quick way of summoning them. From the 1870s the telephone made getting help much quicker. So did people living in growing cities, as this brought them closer to emergency centres.

Police cars must be fast and reliable. Back in 1948 this German Volkswagen fitted the bill.

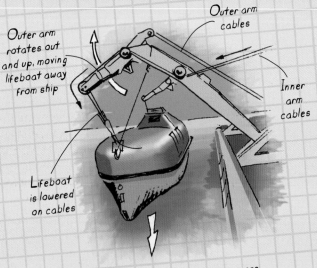

Outer arm cables

Outer arm rotates out and up, moving lifeboat away from ship

Inner arm cables

Lifeboat is lowered on cables

Modern lifeboats ensure that passengers are kept safe and dry in the event of a disaster.

DISASTER AT SEA

The tragic sinking of the huge liner *Titanic* in 1912, which caused the deaths of more than 1500 people, brought great changes to the way people responded to emergencies – especially at sea. From that time all ships had to carry enough lifeboats for everyone on board. They also had to keep their radio room open all day, every day, because the newly invented radio network was the fastest way to call for help if catastrophe struck, and it still is.

MERCY MISSION

Aircraft are much faster than cars or boats. Helicopters in particular need no roads or runways. They are often first to arrive at a disaster scene such as an earthquake zone or flood. Their relief effort brings urgent supplies such as medicines, food and water. The helicopters take away the most seriously injured people – and are soon back again. As road and rail links are repaired, trucks and trains can take over these tasks.

An aid helicopter delivers emergency supplies. Every minute counts, so the ground crew spring into action.

All of the vehicles in this book are Internet linked.
Visit www.factsforprojects.com to find out more.

LAW AND ORDER

Burglary, car theft, noisy neighbours, broken-down trucks, angry fights, road accidents – police officers are called out to attend a range of very different situations. Fast vehicles, expert drivers, flashing lights and wailing sirens mean that their help has arrived. Police organize other emergency services so they all work together. They also tape off the scene, move along bystanders who stop to stare, and make sure that in the confusion, no one tries to commit a crime.

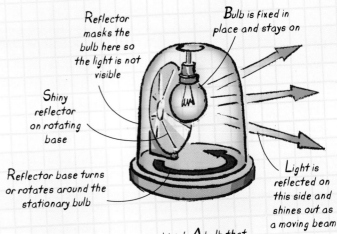

Reflector masks the bulb here so the light is not visible

Bulb is fixed in place and stays on

Shiny reflector on rotating base

Reflector base turns or rotates around the stationary bulb

Light is reflected on this side and shines out as a moving beam

The flashing light is an optical trick. A bulb that really flashed on-off would soon go 'pop'.

Firefighters get as close as possible to assess the blaze, put out the flames and save people and property.

SAVING LIVES

The biggest tragedy is losing a life. The first few seconds and minutes of a medical emergency are the most precious, so paramedics try to get there super-fast. Then the ambulance crews take over and rush the patient to the emergency staff back at the medical centre. All of these highly trained people are dedicated to saving lives, treating injuries and getting patients on the road to recovery.

An ambulance and its crew provide emergency treatment, helping to save a life in the balance.

POLICE MOTORCYCLE

Able to weave through traffic, squeeze along narrow paths and cross rough ground, its engine revving and siren screaming, the police motorcycle is often first to an emergency. Its rider is an expert at assessing the scene in seconds, and then sending radio messages back to base about the situation and which emergency services to summon. The bike is equipped and maintained to the highest standard – and environmentally clean too.

Eureka!

Practical motorcycles went on sale in Europe in 1894. About 14 years later they were in use by police in US cities such as Detroit, Michigan and Portland, Oregon. Their speed through crowded streets meant a boom in crime-solving.

Whatever next?

Jet-powered motorbikes are the fastest two-wheeled vehicles. However control at high speed on a rough surface is a problem.

One of the best-selling items in the famous Lego toy range is its model police motorcycle and rider.

A line of police motorcycles in London, UK

Windshield

Mirror

Light

Fuel tank

Gearbox

✳ In the SADDLE

Police motorcyclists undergo years of training in how to ride fast but safely, and how to get through hold-ups such as traffic jams. They become expert on their favourite machine, and can demonstrate amazing control. But the bike is more than just a way to travel. It is a mini-control centre for organizing help, a carrier of emergency equipment, and a barrier in case of danger such as thrown objects or gunfire.

V-twin Each of the two cylinders has cooling fins (ridges) on the outside and a sliding piston inside. The cylinders are set at an angle to each other in a design known as the V-twin.

To see which models of Harley-Davidson motorcycles are used by some police forces visit www.factsforprojects.com and click on the web link.

The main makes of motorcycle used by police forces worldwide include Harley-Davidson of the USA, BMW of Germany (the chief make in Europe), and the Japanese manufacturers Yamaha, Kawasaki and Honda.

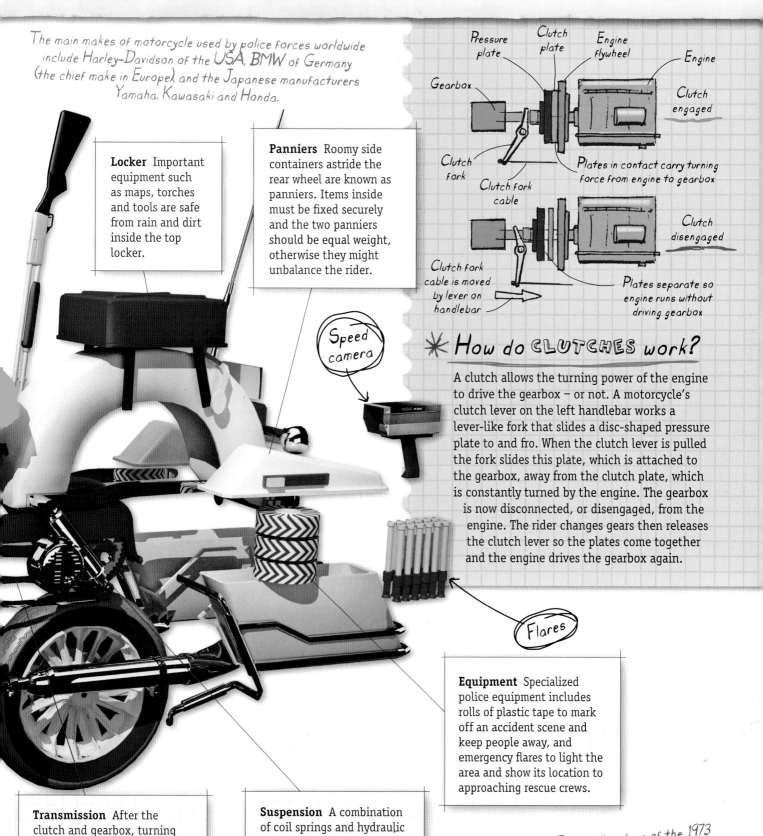

Pressure plate

Clutch plate

Engine flywheel

Engine

Gearbox

Clutch engaged

Clutch fork

Plates in contact carry turning force from engine to gearbox

Clutch fork cable

Clutch disengaged

Clutch fork cable is moved by lever on handlebar

Plates separate so engine runs without driving gearbox

Locker Important equipment such as maps, torches and tools are safe from rain and dirt inside the top locker.

Panniers Roomy side containers astride the rear wheel are known as panniers. Items inside must be fixed securely and the two panniers should be equal weight, otherwise they might unbalance the rider.

Speed camera

Flares

✳ How do CLUTCHES work?

A clutch allows the turning power of the engine to drive the gearbox – or not. A motorcycle's clutch lever on the left handlebar works a lever-like fork that slides a disc-shaped pressure plate to and fro. When the clutch lever is pulled the fork slides this plate, which is attached to the gearbox, away from the clutch plate, which is constantly turned by the engine. The gearbox is now disconnected, or disengaged, from the engine. The rider changes gears then releases the clutch lever so the plates come together and the engine drives the gearbox again.

Equipment Specialized police equipment includes rolls of plastic tape to mark off an accident scene and keep people away, and emergency flares to light the area and show its location to approaching rescue crews.

Transmission After the clutch and gearbox, turning power is taken to the rear wheel either by sprockets and a chain, as on a bicycle, or by a rod-like spinning drive shaft.

Suspension A combination of coil springs and hydraulic dampers let the rear wheel move up and down to absorb road bumps and holes.

One of the stars of the 1973 movie 'Electra Glide in Blue' was the Harley-Davidson motorcyle model named the Electra Glide.

BOMB DISPOSAL ROBOT

Bombs and explosive devices become terrifyingly real when you have to crouch next to one to defuse it. Robots do this without risk to human life. Some disarm the bomb while trying to preserve it, so that experts can learn if the bomb-makers have any new tricks. Others carry the bomb to a safe place where it can be exploded. Most robots are remote controlled by personnel using radio signals from a safe distance.

Many military robots now search for IEDs (improvised explosive devices) – usually roadside bombs.

Eureka!

Bomb disposal began in World War I (1914–18), partly because hastily produced bombs resulted in a higher proportion of duds and unexploded bombs on the battlefield. The first robots arrived in the 1970s to counter the threat of car bombs during The Troubles in Ireland.

Whatever next?

Future robots may be programmed with all the latest tricks so they can predict which booby-traps the bomb-makers will invent next.

One of the top multi-role combat robots is PackBot, with more than 2500 in action worldwide. It has two sets of tracks. Each rear track rotates on flippers in order to climb boulders and stairs.

Sniffers Various specialized sensors detect tiny amounts of substances floating in the air, including explosive chemicals. Different sensors are fitted depending on the chemicals suspected.

☀ How do TRACKS steer?

Caterpillar or crawler tracks are used in many vehicles, from bomb disposal robots to giant tanks, bulldozers, diggers and other construction machines. Their many shoes, or plates, grip well and also spread the weight so the vehicle does not sink into soft ground and get stuck. The speeds of the two tracks are controlled separately, often by two handles or levers worked by the driver. Making one track turn faster than the other causes the vehicle to steer to the opposite side.

Electric drive system Most robots have electric motors to work the tracks and also the on-board arms and levers. The track ones are known as traction or propulsion motors and are slow-spinning but with huge turning power.

Drive wheel Usually only one wheel on each side is turned by the motor to move the track. The track itself then spins the other wheels.

Return roller

Teeth

Road wheels The road wheels are allowed to turn at their own speed on their own axles, while distributing the robot's weight along the track.

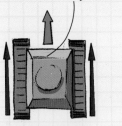

Both tracks running at the same speed move the vehicle forwards in a straight line

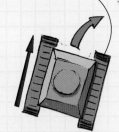

Speeding up the left track turns the vehicle to the right

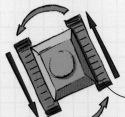

If one track is driven forward, and the other drives in reverse, the vehicle spins around on the spot

Watch a video of PackBot in action by visiting
www.factsforprojects.com and clicking on the web link.

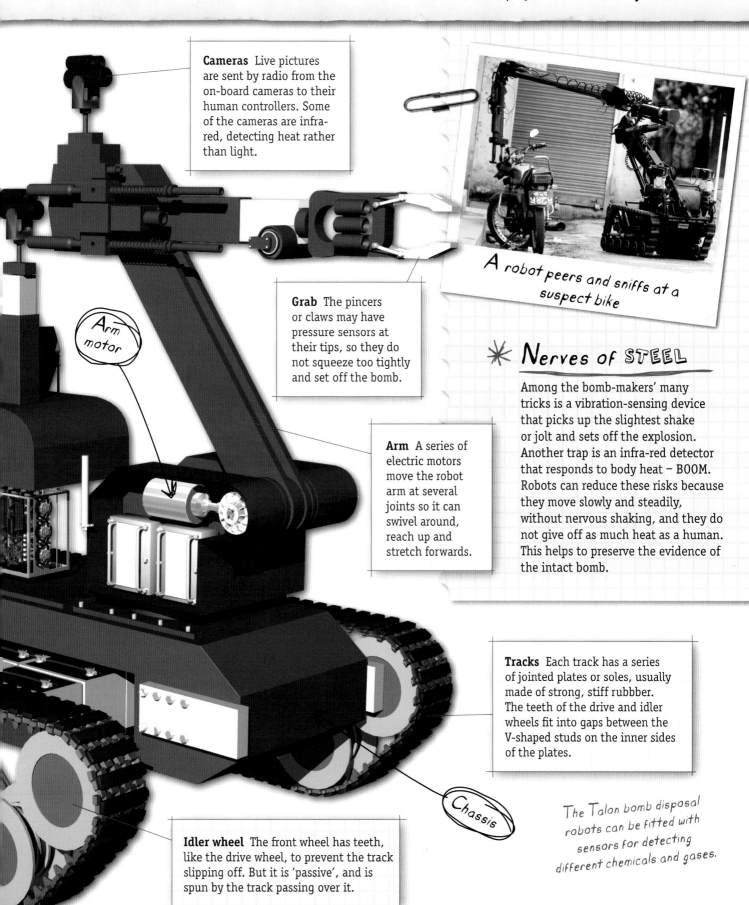

Cameras Live pictures are sent by radio from the on-board cameras to their human controllers. Some of the cameras are infra-red, detecting heat rather than light.

A robot peers and sniffs at a suspect bike

Arm motor

Grab The pincers or claws may have pressure sensors at their tips, so they do not squeeze too tightly and set off the bomb.

Arm A series of electric motors move the robot arm at several joints so it can swivel around, reach up and stretch forwards.

Nerves of STEEL

Among the bomb-makers' many tricks is a vibration-sensing device that picks up the slightest shake or jolt and sets off the explosion. Another trap is an infra-red detector that responds to body heat – BOOM. Robots can reduce these risks because they move slowly and steadily, without nervous shaking, and they do not give off as much heat as a human. This helps to preserve the evidence of the intact bomb.

Tracks Each track has a series of jointed plates or soles, usually made of strong, stiff rubbber. The teeth of the drive and idler wheels fit into gaps between the V-shaped studs on the inner sides of the plates.

Chassis

The Talon bomb disposal robots can be fitted with sensors for detecting different chemicals and gases.

Idler wheel The front wheel has teeth, like the drive wheel, to prevent the track slipping off. But it is 'passive', and is spun by the track passing over it.

POLICE PATROL CAR

A part from cruising highways to ensure that motorists drive more carefully, police vehicles also dash to road traffic accidents and other emergencies. The modern patrol car is packed with cameras, computers and other electronic gadgets. It has direct radio links to the regional control room and the computer databases for stolen or suspect vehicles and for people on the wanted list.

Eureka!

In 1899 the first police car went on patrol in Akron, Ohio, USA. It was powered by an electric motor and had a top speed of 26 kilometres per hour. Its first call was to pick up a drunken man on Main Street!

Whatever next?

The taser is a high-voltage dart on a long wire, fired at people to shock them out of troublesome behaviour. Versions are being tested that may be able to disable speeding or stolen cars.

The automatic number plate recognition identifies almost any car and its owner within a few seconds.

Dashboard computer The latest laptop links into the car's many computer systems for instant display of roads, suspects and other information.

Bull bars The reinforced front guards or fenders are able to push other cars or knock down doors without damage to the car itself.

Flashing lights

Camera

Wing mirrors

POLICE

V8 engine

✳ How do FLASHING LIGHTS work?

The 'flashing light' on many emergency vehicles works in various ways. In one design the light does not flash at all – it is a bulb that glows continuously. A shiny bowl-shaped reflector turns around it, making the bulb's beam whirl around. To an onlooker it appears to flash. This method overcomes the problem of burning out the bulb with continual flashes, and twisting its wires if the bulb itself spun around.

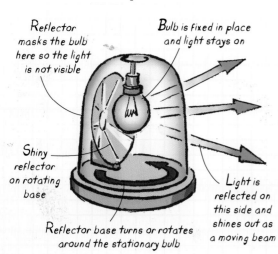

Reflector masks the bulb here so the light is not visible

Bulb is fixed in place and light stays on

Shiny reflector on rotating base

Light is reflected on this side and shines out as a moving beam

Reflector base turns or rotates around the stationary bulb

Learn more about the unique features of police patrol cars by visiting www.factsforprojects.com and clicking on the web link.

Disc drives On-board computer hard discs carry the latest information about stolen cars and wanted criminals, in case the patrol car's radio links are damaged or out of range.

Antenna (aerial) Much of the officers' work relies on them staying in contact with headquarters. So the car has several antennae to cope with different signal strengths and wavelengths according to radio conditions.

Stinger Stowed neatly in its box, the spiky stinger can be unloaded and unrolled in a few seconds (see below).

Italian motorway police have the world's fastest patrol cars – three ultra-speedy Lamborghini Gallardos. They can travel at over 300 km/h but rarely do. Their main duties are escorting medical emergencies and supplies, and raising awareness of motorway patrols. However one was 'totalled' (destroyed) in a crash in November 2009.

5 PCT 2582

COURTESY
PROFESSIONALISM
RESPECT

NYPD

Disc brake

Chassis

Graphic markings Patrol cars must show their police force or department, unless the officers are working in secret or undercover, in which case they may be in an ordinary-looking 'unmarked car'.

✴ You've been STUNG!

The stinger or traffic spike strip is a row of sharp metal spikes unrolled across a roadway, sharp points upwards. Its aim is to puncture the tyres of a suspect vehicle passing over it. The spike design varies. Some shapes allow the tyres to go down gradually, so that the driver does not suffer four sudden 'blow-outs' and lose control. But this does not always work, giving the stinger the nickname of 'tyre-shredder'.

A stinger is rolled up again after use

PARAMEDIC MOTORCYCLE

Like a micro ambulance on two wheels, the paramedic bike has emergency equipment and medication for the most life-threatening injuries and illnesses. The paramedic rider is trained not just in first aid but in many detailed procedures such as giving oxygen and and heart defibrillation (using a controlled electric shock to restore a normal heart rhythm).

Paramedic bikes may be used to rush human organs, such as hearts for transplant, to hospitals.

Eureka!

'Motorcycle ambulances' ridden by trained medics began saving lives during World War I (1914–18). But equipment such as defibrillators has only been portable and tough enough for on-site use since the 1980s.

Whatever next?

Heart monitors and similar gadgets send their readouts by radio to the nearest medical centre, where doctors advise the paramedic on urgent action.

Fairing

After a motorcyle accident, the paramedic arrives in less than three minutes

✳ FIRST on the SCENE

After a heart attack, stroke or similar event, the faster treatment comes, the greater the chances of saving life and a much improved outcome. The first 'platinum ten minutes' is when the paramedic and the kit carried on the bike can make so much difference, after speeding through traffic or along narrow lanes. The first hour is also known as the 'golden hour' – again, a vital time to identify the problem and give medication. When the ambulance arrives, it has more equipment and it can take the patient to hospital.

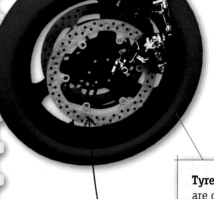

Front forks

Disc brake

Tyres The tubeless tyres are checked daily for the correct air pressure inside. Wrong pressure can make them wear too fast or unevenly and reduce their grip on the road surface.

To watch a video of a paramedic motorcycle in action visit www.factsforprojects.com and click on the web link.

Medication pack Various medicines and drugs are stowed in one pannier. They are always checked, replaced and updated as necessary after each trip.

Cardiac monitor The heart monitor shows a wavy line or trace, the ECG (electrocardiogram). This gives clues to the patient's health and whether a defibrillator is needed to 'shock' the heart back into a normal beating rhythm.

Oxygen Breathing difficulties are eased by oxygen from the cylinder delivered through a face mask. Pain-killing gases can also be given this way.

Fire extinguisher

Fluid packs Inside the containers are various types of blood replacement fluids, as well as medications already dissolved in liquid, perhaps to be administered through a 'drip' directly into a vein.

✳ How do TUBELESS TYRES work?

Inner tubes can cause problems if punctured – such as bursting like a balloon. A tubeless tyre, with no separate inner tube, is more likely to deflate gradually if punctured. The tubeless tyre's edges are two rounded rubber beads, each with a strong steel cable inside for strength. High pressure from the air in the tyre keeps each bead pressed against a recess in the wheel rim, for an airtight seal.

Some giant shopping malls and sports stadiums have indoor electric paramedic scooters. Noisy petrol engines would pollute the air with their dangerous exhaust fumes.

Tread
Rubber tyre
High pressure air
Air pressure keeps tyre hard and bead pressed onto wheel rim
High tensile steel wire inside tyre bead
Bead seating recess on metal wheel rim
Wheel rim
Wheel spokes

AMBULANCE

Ambulance drivers need a careful combination of speed and safety as they race to an emergency, sirens and lights warning other motorists to pull over. The vehicle contains the most important medical machines and drugs for critical cases. It also acts as a shelter where people who feel sick or faint can rest and be monitored, hopefully to recover.

Eureka!

Since the 14th century, horse-drawn wagons transported the injured and sick to the nearest physician – or mortuary. As these wagons evolved, they carried pills and potions to treat the casualties. The first motorized ambulance was used in 1899 in Chicago. From 1909 onwards they were mass produced.

Whatever next?

Advances in electronics mean that smarter heart and brain monitors analyze their own readings and help ambulance staff to identify illness.

Giant bus ambulances in Dubai can treat more than 50 patients.

Medical supplies The array of medications, usually kept in a locked cupboard, can treat most types of emergencies.

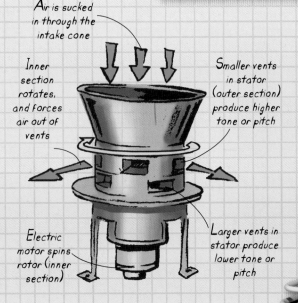

Air is sucked in through the intake cone

Inner section rotates, and forces air out of vents

Smaller vents in stator (outer section) produce higher tone or pitch

Electric motor spins rotor (inner section)

Larger vents in stator produce lower tone or pitch

✳ How do SIRENS work?

The pneumatic or air-based two-tone siren produces the familiar 'na-na-na-na' sound. An electric motor spins a collar-like inner section called the rotor within an outer stationary cylinder, the stator. The shape of the rotor sucks in air and blasts it out through vents in the stator. The spinning rotor alternately blocks then uncovers the vents in the stator, forcing out bursts of air, which are rapidly squeezed and stretched to make soundwaves. The rotor speed controls the overall pitch, high or low.

Stretcher The fold-away stretcher can be adjusted for height, depending on the patient's treatment.

Fuel tank

Take a virtual tour of an ambulance by visiting
www.factsforprojects.com and clicking on the web link.

The latest mobile X-ray units are smaller than a shoebox.

Medic

✳ Coming THROUGH!

Many emergency vehicles have flashing lights and wailing sirens to tell others of their urgent missions. Many kinds of sirens have been designed, but one problem is that in city streets lined by tall buildings, the siren's noise bounces around. This means motorists and other people cannot tell from which direction the ambulance is coming. So new types of sirens are continually being tested, as well as multi-sirens that keep changing their beeps and wails.

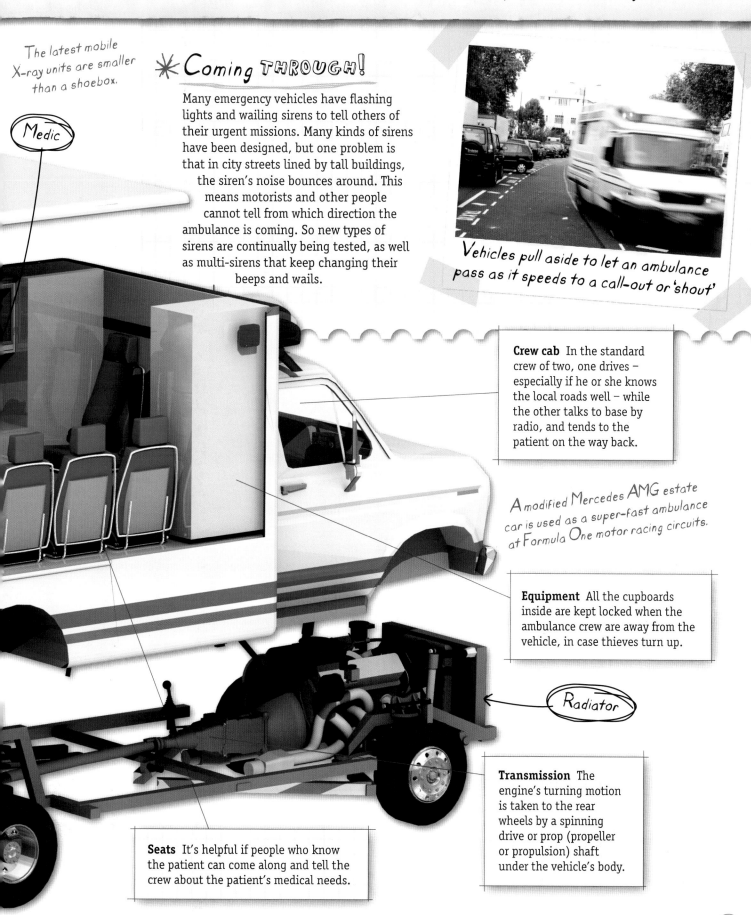

Vehicles pull aside to let an ambulance pass as it speeds to a call-out or 'shout'

Crew cab In the standard crew of two, one drives – especially if he or she knows the local roads well – while the other talks to base by radio, and tends to the patient on the way back.

A modified Mercedes AMG estate car is used as a super-fast ambulance at Formula One motor racing circuits.

Equipment All the cupboards inside are kept locked when the ambulance crew are away from the vehicle, in case thieves turn up.

Radiator

Transmission The engine's turning motion is taken to the rear wheels by a spinning drive or prop (propeller or propulsion) shaft under the vehicle's body.

Seats It's helpful if people who know the patient can come along and tell the crew about the patient's medical needs.

OFFROAD RESCUE TRUCK

Emergencies do not always happen next to smooth roads. Out in the wild, climbers, trekkers and cavers run risks – and rely on off-roaders if there is an emergency. These vehicles have extra-strong suspension, extra-grip tyres, and extra-high ground clearance, which is the gap between the lowest part of the vehicle and the surface below.

Eureka!

Informal mountain rescue, by friends or local volunteers, has been around for centuries. Organized rescue teams began in the 1900s, with pack animals such as horses, mules or llamas. Motor vehicles became rugged enough to be used in the 1920s.

Whatever next?

Floating air-cushion vehicles – hovercraft – have been tested in remote rescue situations, but they are usually too difficult to control.

Fuel and water cans

The first Jeeps were built in 1940 for US military use.

The first Land Rovers were stars of the 1948 Amsterdam Motor Show in the Netherlands.

Roof rack Bulky but fairly lightweight items are carried here. Many mounting points (supports) spread the weight of the load around the whole roof area.

A Land Rover takes a steep, bumpy track in its stride

✳ OLD but RELIABLE

The Jeep and then the Land Rover vehicles date back to the 1940s. Inspired by the need to carry troops, supplies and casualties over rough ground in warfare, the Jeep quickly set the standard for toughness and ease of repair as a 4WD ATV (four-wheel-drive all-terrain vehicle). The Land Rover took the idea onto civilian roads with its simple design and fewer parts to go wrong. The steel-based chassis and the body parts made of aluminium-based alloys (combinations of metals) mean strength, lightness and no rusting.

Emergency equipment A first-aid paramedic pack of medicines, drugs and dressings, a lightweight carry-stretcher and other medical supplies are taken to most emergencies.

Mud flap

Steps

Flares

Chassis The main framework, or chassis, has very stiff, extra-strong metal beams or members compared to most road vehicles.

Stiffened suspension

Find out how mountain rescue teams operate by visiting
www.factsforprojects.com and clicking on the web link.

The original Land Rovers are tough but not especially quiet or comfortable. So the company makes more luxurious 4WD models such as the Discovery and Freelander.

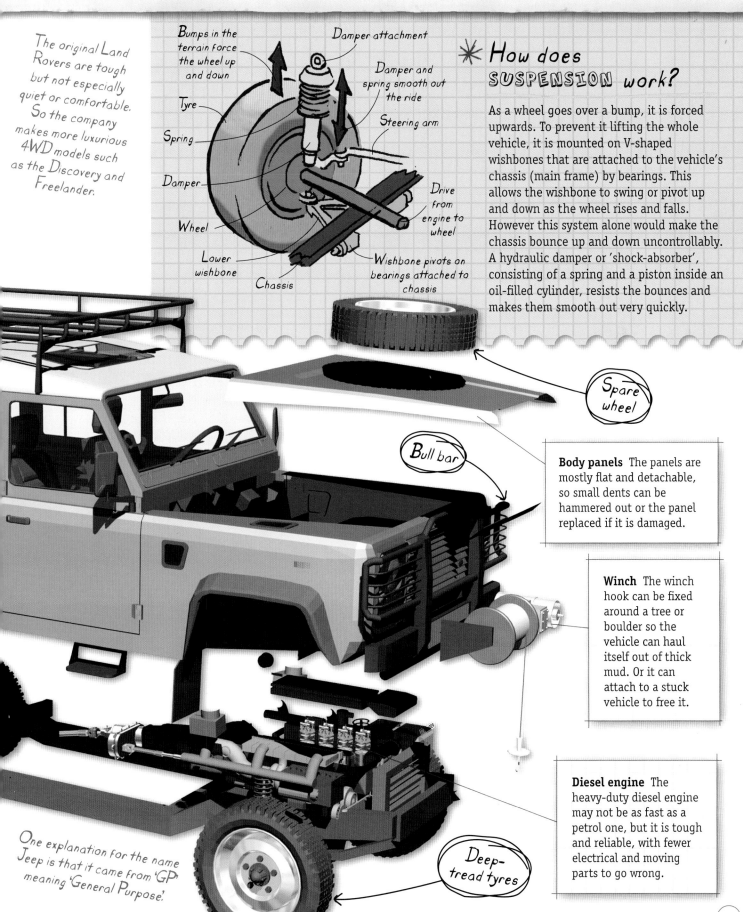

Bumps in the terrain force the wheel up and down

Damper attachment

Damper and spring smooth out the ride

Steering arm

Tyre

Spring

Damper

Drive from engine to wheel

Wheel

Lower wishbone

Chassis

Wishbone pivots on bearings attached to chassis

How does SUSPENSION work?

As a wheel goes over a bump, it is forced upwards. To prevent it lifting the whole vehicle, it is mounted on V-shaped wishbones that are attached to the vehicle's chassis (main frame) by bearings. This allows the wishbone to swing or pivot up and down as the wheel rises and falls. However this system alone would make the chassis bounce up and down uncontrollably. A hydraulic damper or 'shock-absorber', consisting of a spring and a piston inside an oil-filled cylinder, resists the bounces and makes them smooth out very quickly.

Spare wheel

Bull bar

Body panels The panels are mostly flat and detachable, so small dents can be hammered out or the panel replaced if it is damaged.

Winch The winch hook can be fixed around a tree or boulder so the vehicle can haul itself out of thick mud. Or it can attach to a stuck vehicle to free it.

Diesel engine The heavy-duty diesel engine may not be as fast as a petrol one, but it is tough and reliable, with fewer electrical and moving parts to go wrong.

Deep-tread tyres

One explanation for the name Jeep is that it came from 'GP' meaning 'General Purpose'.

19

FIRE TENDER

The fire tender doesn't just fight fires. It is an all-round emergency vehicle central to many kinds of incidents, from putting out unwanted campfires to assisting in major disasters such as earthquakes or explosions. Apart from the water pumps and hoses, its array of tools and equipment includes hammers, saws, chisels and cutters. It also has powerful lights for work at night or in dark places such as tunnels and underpasses.

Eureka!

Mechanical water pumps for fire tenders date back to the 18th century. The tender at that time was horsedrawn, the pump was human-powered. People pushed up and down on a large lever pivoted at its centre, like a see-saw.

Whatever next?

The flexible materials for hoses are continually being improved. A burst through a small crack could seriously injure someone nearby.

Emergency horns

Driver and co-driver cab
The driver uses all kinds of modern aids including satnav or GPS to find the best big-vehicle route to the emergency.

Radiator grille

Road horns

✳ How does a RADIATOR work?

Petrol and diesel engines continually explode fuel inside, so they make huge amounts of heat. To prevent this causing damage, a coolant – mainly water plus anti-freeze chemicals – flows through a system of channels and spaces in the engine and takes in the heat. Its circuit continues into the metal radiator, which has hundreds of tiny flaps, or vanes, specialized to give off heat to the air around.

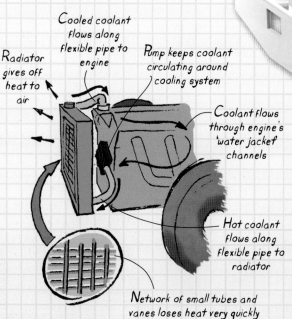

Cooled coolant flows along flexible pipe to engine

Pump keeps coolant circulating around cooling system

Radiator gives off heat to air

Coolant flows through engine's 'water jacket' channels

Hot coolant flows along flexible pipe to radiator

Network of small tubes and vanes loses heat very quickly

The fastest working fire-fighting vehicle is a Nissan R35 Skyline car fitted with a large extinguisher tank in place of the rear seats. At the Nurburgring raceway near Cologne, Germany it puts out accidental fires and makes fuel spills safe.

Powerful engine Water and tools are very heavy, so a big fire tender ready to tackle a blaze may weigh more than 20 tonnes. This can limit its movements, for example, across small or weak bridges.

Take a virtual tour of a fire tender by visiting
www.factsforprojects.com and clicking on the web link.

Exhausts Dangerous exhaust fumes are released above head height to avoid affecting the crew.

Ladders

Suits and breathing gear Specialized flameproof suits and breathing equipment are stowed in the forward lockers.

Firefighting motorcycles carry fire blankets, extinguishers and foam guns.

Tool lockers The tools and equipment are packed away in the same place every time, so the crew know exactly how to reach them fast.

Deluge gun

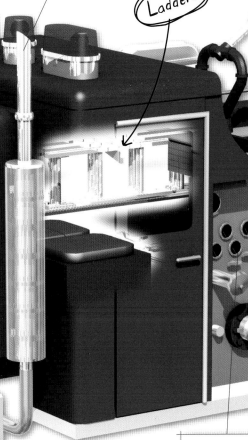

Gauges and controls The various water pumps, foam pumps and hydraulic gear such as spreaders are controlled from one main panel.

Water tanks Standard tenders hold around 2000 to 5000 litres of water plus containers of foam concentrate.

Specialized fire equipment includes turntable ladders, foam sprayers, water tanker trucks and 'cherry-picker' hydraulic platforms.

Holding the hose needs training for skill as well as strength

✳ Under PRESSURE

Enormous pressure is needed to make water shoot 50 metres or more onto the heart of a fire. As the water blasts forwards, it produces a reaction – an equal force in the opposite direction, causing the hose to jump backwards. Teams of firefighters brace themselves as the pressure is slowly turned up, to resist the reaction force and keep the hose steady. A dropped hose thrashes about on the ground, and the water pressure must be turned down before the team can get hold of it again.

AIRPORT FIRE-CRASH TENDER

One of the most intense emergencies is an aircraft fire. More than 500 people may be trapped inside the long metal tube of the fuselage, with hundreds of tonnes of highly flammable jet fuel all around. For major airports, regulations state that airport fire tenders – which can weigh more than 40 tonnes – must be at the scene, pumping foam, within two minutes. If the tenders are not available, for whatever reason, then no planes can take off or land.

Eureka!

Chemical fire-fighting foams were first developed in the late 19th century. They were mainly for fires at factories and depots handling petrol-type fuels for the rapidly growing car market.

Whatever next?

Putting out flames means starving them of oxygen in the air, which they need for burning. Very heavy inert gases can produce an invisible blanket to do this.

One of the main dry chemical fire-retarding powders is known as Purple K for its added violet dye colour.

Cannon The foam or water 'gun' is known as a cannon or monitor. It is aimed by the operator or co-driver inside the cab.

✳ How do PUNCTURE NOZZLES work?

If fuel leaks into an aircraft cabin, there is a massive risk that it may catch fire or even explode in a fireball. The puncture or piercing nozzle is a new system carried by some fire-crash tenders. A sharp nozzle on a telescopic arm can extend up to 20 metres from the tender and punch itself through the metal fuselage. A harmless chemical fire retardant is then pumped along the arm and through the nozzle into the inside of the fuselage.

Cab There may be room for five or more crew in the cab. Often there is an engineer who is an expert on the plane involved. He or she gives advice about danger points such as where the plane's fuel pipes run.

Heat-resistant bodywork

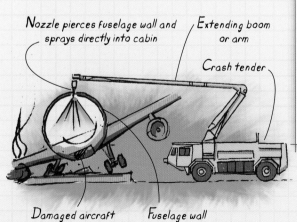

Nozzle pierces fuselage wall and sprays directly into cabin

Extending boom or arm

Crash tender

Damaged aircraft

Fuselage wall

A big airport tender may carry 15,000 litres of water, 2400 litres of foam chemicals and 200 kg of firefighting dry chemicals.

Watch a video of an airport fire-crash tender in action by visiting www.factsforprojects.com and clicking on the web link.

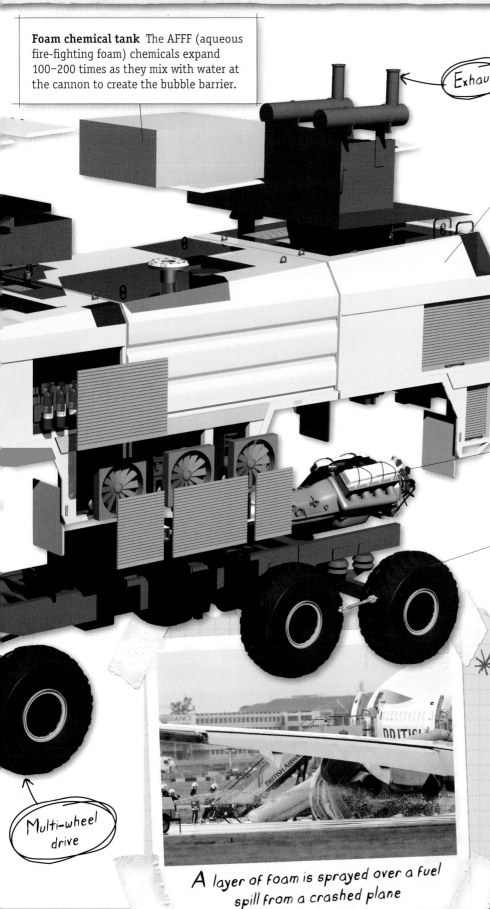

Foam chemical tank The AFFF (aqueous fire-fighting foam) chemicals expand 100–200 times as they mix with water at the cannon to create the bubble barrier.

Exhaust

Tool racks Many of the tools are similar to those in a standard fire tender (see previous page), such as hydraulic cutters worked by high-pressure oil pumps driven by the vehicle's engine.

Airport tenders must have regular checks to see how long it takes them to race to the farthest corners of the airport.

Engine Such a massive vehicle, probably weighing more than 40 tonnes, needs a huge V8 turbodiesel engine to accelerate it to the crash site.

Tyres An aircraft emergency may happen anywhere at the airfield or airport. The tender must be able to cross grassy and rough areas with its low-pressure, high-grip tyres.

Multi-wheel drive

✳ Under the BLANKET

Water puts out many kinds of fires. But on flaming liquid fuels it mixes and flares up, creating yet more danger. Chemical foams called fire retardants are used instead. Two chemicals are mixed with water as they spray from the hose or cannon (monitor) to make a mass of bubbles that keep air away from the flammable liquid. Fuel tanks in the plane and fuel leaks or spills on the ground are all covered with a blanket of foam to prevent more flames.

A layer of foam is sprayed over a fuel spill from a crashed plane

FIREBOAT

Not just able to tackle fires and other emergencies on boats and ships, but also on oil rigs, dams, bridges, at waterfront warehouses, along harbours, ports and docks – the fireboat is an adaptable floating firefighter. This craft is often combined with a rescue vessel and first aid centre. Its massively powerful water/foam cannons, or monitors, can spray more than 100 metres.

Eureka!

In the 19th century steam-powered boats were adapted to spray water using steam-driven pumps. London's first self-propelled fireboat *Alpha II* went into service in 1900, and many other ports quickly followed.

Whatever next?

Taller booms are being developed that will allow water to be sprayed down into the centre or seat of the fire. This is much more effective at dousing flames.

The Warner L Lawrence fireboat in Los Angeles, USA, can spray water more than 120 m up into the air.

Bridge The captain controls all aspects of the boat from this main control room. There are wrap-around windows for a wide view and radio communications with the boat's other rooms and crew members, including the firefighters.

Radar

Radio antennae

Deck water/ foam cannon The forward deck-mounted cannon (monitor) is aimed at lower areas of a blaze.

Cannon deck

Lifebelts

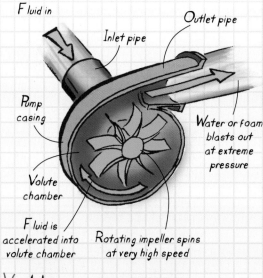

Fluid in

Inlet pipe

Outlet pipe

Pump casing

Water or foam blasts out at extreme pressure

Volute chamber

Fluid is accelerated into volute chamber

Rotating impeller spins at very high speed

✳ How do HIGH-PRESSURE PUMPS work?

One of the main high-pressure pumps for fluids – gases and liquids – is the centrifugal pump. Its rotating impeller is similar to an aircraft propeller but with blades that are slightly bent and not set at an angle. The impeller is spun at high speed by an electric motor, diesel or petrol engine, or steam turbine, and draws in fluid near its centre. The rotating blades fling the fluid outwards with so-called centrifugal force, into a doughnut-shaped space around – the volute chamber. Here, the peaks of pressure even out as the blades pass, and the fluid is forced away at steady pressure through the outlet.

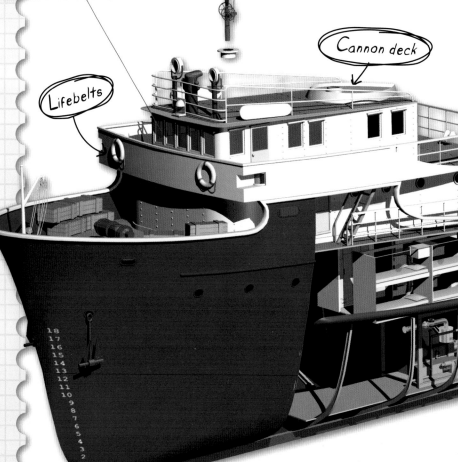

To see a video of a fireboat in action visit
www.factsforprojects.com and click on the web link.

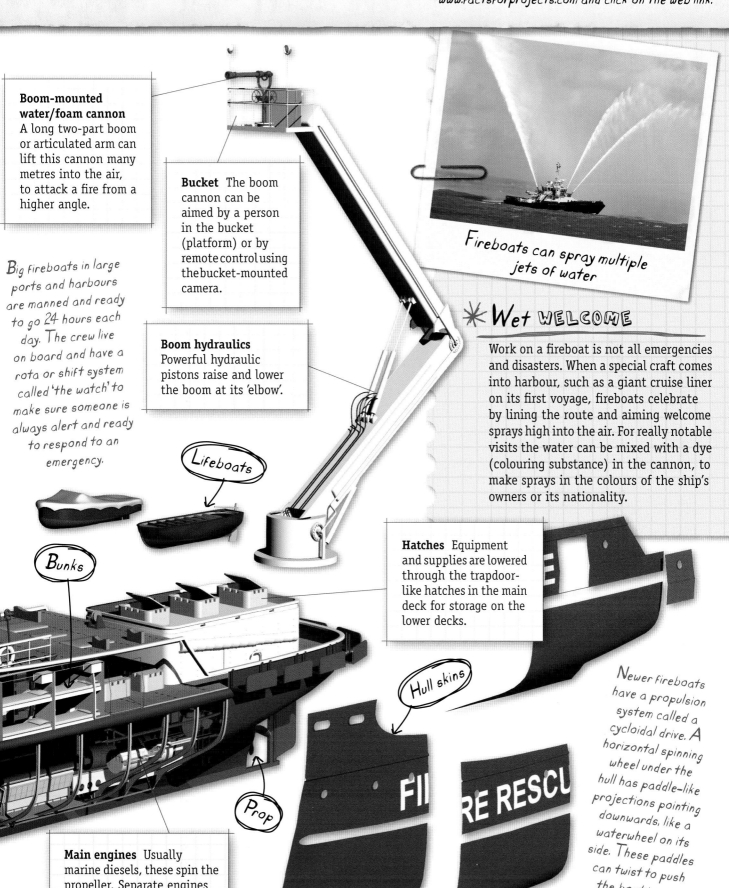

Fireboats can spray multiple jets of water

Boom-mounted water/foam cannon
A long two-part boom or articulated arm can lift this cannon many metres into the air, to attack a fire from a higher angle.

Big fireboats in large ports and harbours are manned and ready to go 24 hours each day. The crew live on board and have a rota or shift system called 'the watch' to make sure someone is always alert and ready to respond to an emergency.

Bucket The boom cannon can be aimed by a person in the bucket (platform) or by remote control using the bucket-mounted camera.

Boom hydraulics
Powerful hydraulic pistons raise and lower the boom at its 'elbow'.

Lifeboats

Bunks

✳ Wet WELCOME

Work on a fireboat is not all emergencies and disasters. When a special craft comes into harbour, such as a giant cruise liner on its first voyage, fireboats celebrate by lining the route and aiming welcome sprays high into the air. For really notable visits the water can be mixed with a dye (colouring substance) in the cannon, to make sprays in the colours of the ship's owners or its nationality.

Hatches Equipment and supplies are lowered through the trapdoor-like hatches in the main deck for storage on the lower decks.

Hull skins

FIRE RESCU

Prop

Main engines Usually marine diesels, these spin the propeller. Separate engines power the cannons.

Newer fireboats have a propulsion system called a cycloidal drive. A horizontal spinning wheel under the hull has paddle-like projections pointing downwards, like a waterwheel on its side. These paddles can twist to push the boat in any direction.

SHIP'S LIFEBOAT

For most people, lifeboats are never used, and stay as a comforting reminder that help is at hand should storms and rough seas strike. If the lifeboat is ever launched, it becomes a survival centre for all those on board. It must be strong and tough, with unsinkable construction, able to withstand high winds and ride out big waves, as well as provide shelter and supplies until rescue vessels reach the scene.

Eureka!

More than 3000 years ago, ancient Phoenician boats carried small wooden life rafts. International rules controlling lifeboats were strengthened following the tragic sinking of *RMS Titanic* in 1912. The giant liner carried more than 3000 people but had lifeboat spaces for only 1200.

Whatever next?

New lifeboats carry EPIRBs, or emergency position-indicating beacons – small devices that send out radio signals. Satellites detect these and inform the rescue services of the beacon's location.

Lifeboat drill (practice) is a familiar part of long-distance ship trips. Each person must go to a particular lifeboat position or station.

A life raft inflates its ring-like body first, then the canopy

✳ Space-saving SURVIVAL

Life rafts are blow-up or fold-out types of lifeboats. Their main advantage is that they save space on the ship, and they can also be stowed away in an aircraft in case it has to land or 'ditch' in water. Inflatable types blow up from compressed gas in a high-pressure canister or cylinder. As this happens the emergency radio beacon switches on to send out its locating signals. Life rafts do not have motors and propellers, but they often have oars or paddles. Modern lifeboats may well have a small engine.

Raised bridge The person in charge of the lifeboat – usually a crew member – can see the surroundings and steer from here, as well as keep a check on the engine.

Engine A small marine diesel engine provides power in some lifeboats. This allows the crew to steer away from dangers such as jagged rocks or sandbanks out at sea.

Radio equipment

Drinking water

Rudder

Ballast tanks When the lifeboat is launched, these chambers in the bottom of the hull automatically fill with water. This provides weight or ballast low down, which makes the boat stable and stops it tipping over.

Watch an animation of the new Torpedo lifeboat by visiting www.factsforprojects.com and clicking on the web link.

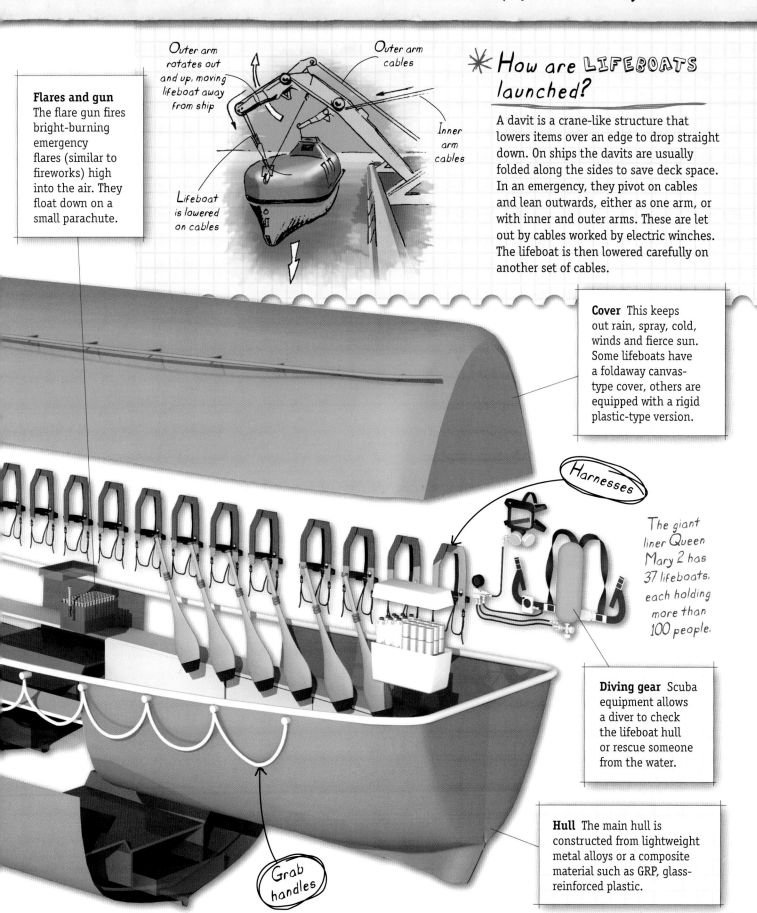

Outer arm rotates out and up, moving lifeboat away from ship

Outer arm cables

Inner arm cables

Lifeboat is lowered on cables

Flares and gun
The flare gun fires bright-burning emergency flares (similar to fireworks) high into the air. They float down on a small parachute.

✳ How are LIFEBOATS launched?

A davit is a crane-like structure that lowers items over an edge to drop straight down. On ships the davits are usually folded along the sides to save deck space. In an emergency, they pivot on cables and lean outwards, either as one arm, or with inner and outer arms. These are let out by cables worked by electric winches. The lifeboat is then lowered carefully on another set of cables.

Cover This keeps out rain, spray, cold, winds and fierce sun. Some lifeboats have a foldaway canvas-type cover, others are equipped with a rigid plastic-type version.

Harnesses

The giant liner Queen Mary 2 has 37 lifeboats, each holding more than 100 people.

Diving gear Scuba equipment allows a diver to check the lifeboat hull or rescue someone from the water.

Grab handles

Hull The main hull is constructed from lightweight metal alloys or a composite material such as GRP, glass-reinforced plastic.

OFFSHORE LIFEBOAT

If a ship gets into trouble at sea, conditions are probably already difficult, with strong winds and crashing waves. Offshore lifeboats must withstand these problems, and more, to carry out their missions as the crew push their craft to its limits. One of the most important features is self-righting (see panel below), when a lifeboat that is tipped over by a giant wave turns to become upright again.

The person in charge of the offshore lifeboat is called the coxwain. There is usually a second coxwain who can take over when needed.

Eureka!

The world's oldest lifeboat organization is the UK's RNLI, Royal National Lifeboat Institution. It was founded in 1824 and on average carries out more than 20 rescues every day.

Whatever next?

Amphibious rescue craft are being tested along swampy areas of coastline where neither boats nor all-terrain vehicles can go.

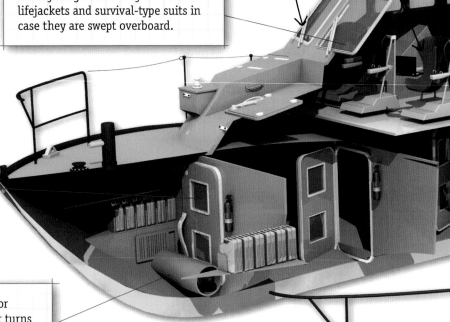

Sprung seats

Wipers

Bridge and cabin The crew may have to strap themselves into their seats in very rough seas. They all wear lifejackets and survival-type suits in case they are swept overboard.

Bulkheads A series of cross-walls or bulkheads from the bow (front) to the stern (rear) divide the boat into a row of watertight compartments. Closing the door seals off each compartment. If one compartment leaks, the water cannot spread into the others.

Bow thrusters A small propellor or water-jet on each side at the front turns the bow left or right, for manoeuvring in tight corners or keeping the boat steady in strong currents and tides.

1. Full ballast tank keeps weight low and lifeboat stable

Righting tank *Ballast tank*

2. A big wave knocks the boat over and water starts to flow into the righting tank

3. The weight of water in the righting tank keeps the boat turning

Ballast tank tips boat

4. After almost a full turn water in the righting tank flows into the ballast tank again

✳ How does SELF-RIGHTING work?

One method for self-righting involves a ballast tank and one or more off-centre righting tanks. Normally the weight of water in the very low ballast tank, in the bottom of the hull, keeps the lifeboat floating upright. If it tilts, this water flows into a righting tank, which puts the lifeboat off balance and makes it continue to spin around. The only stable position is when all the water flows once again into the ballast tank.

The RNLI's Severn Class lifeboats are 17 m long and weigh around 40 tonnes.

Read facts, watch videos and view photos of offshore lifeboats by going to www.factsforprojects.com and clicking on the web link.

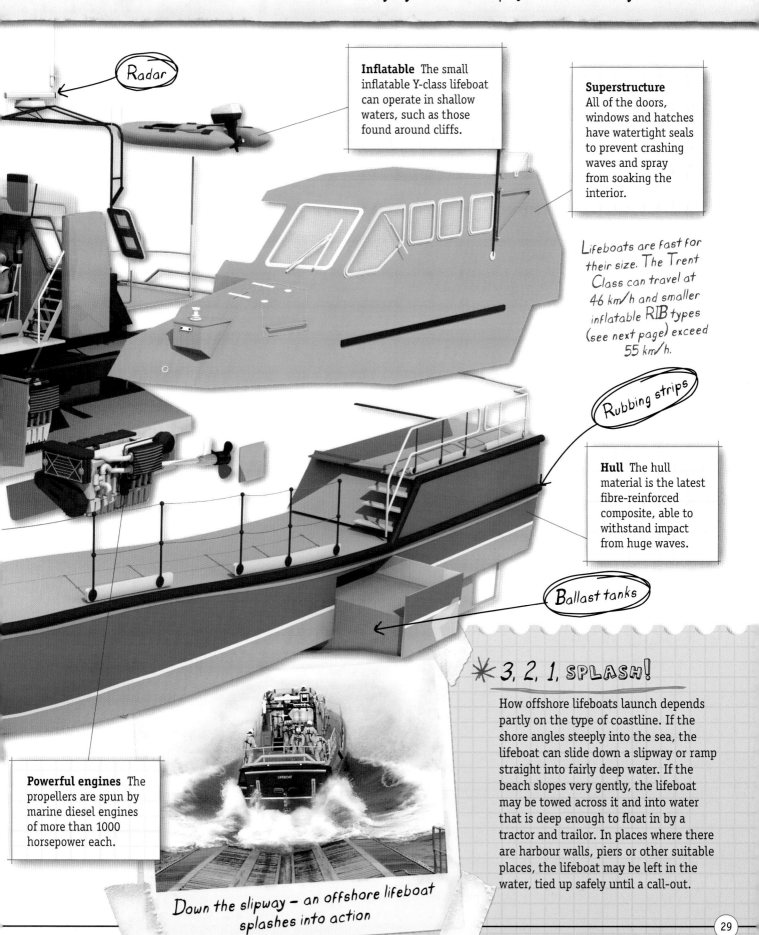

Radar

Inflatable The small inflatable Y-class lifeboat can operate in shallow waters, such as those found around cliffs.

Superstructure All of the doors, windows and hatches have watertight seals to prevent crashing waves and spray from soaking the interior.

Lifeboats are fast for their size. The Trent Class can travel at 46 km/h and smaller inflatable RIB types (see next page) exceed 55 km/h.

Rubbing strips

Hull The hull material is the latest fibre-reinforced composite, able to withstand impact from huge waves.

Ballast tanks

Powerful engines The propellers are spun by marine diesel engines of more than 1000 horsepower each.

Down the slipway – an offshore lifeboat splashes into action

✴ 3, 2, 1, SPLASH!

How offshore lifeboats launch depends partly on the type of coastline. If the shore angles steeply into the sea, the lifeboat can slide down a slipway or ramp straight into fairly deep water. If the beach slopes very gently, the lifeboat may be towed across it and into water that is deep enough to float in by a tractor and trailor. In places where there are harbour walls, piers or other suitable places, the lifeboat may be left in the water, tied up safely until a call-out.

COASTGUARD PATROL BOAT

Bad weather does not stop coastguards responding to an emergency. Their roles vary from country to country, but most will rush to help craft and people in trouble, often assisting the lifeboats. In some countries the coastguards enforce the law too, as they tackle smugglers, illegal fishing and modern-day pirates.

Eureka!

Coastguards are sometimes called the 'fourth emergency service' after police, ambulance and firefighting. National coastguards were set up from about 1800, chiefly to control the boom in smuggling.

Whatever next?

Some coastguard forces have tested underwater pursuit craft such as small submarines, which can follow illegal craft, video their crimes and catch them red-handed.

The USA has more than 70 Marine Protector Class patrol boats. Each is 27 m long, 5.9 m wide and travels at a top speed of 46 km/h.

The 90-tonne Marine Protector patrols have enough supplies for the ten crew to stay at sea for five days. The boat can travel more than 1000 km before needing to refuel.

Speakers It's often noisy at sea, with whooshing winds and crashing waves. But the powerful loudspeakers allow the crew to 'hail' or call to people on nearby vessels.

A patrol boat endures high seas

Gun mounts Machine guns on swivel mountings allow trained crew members to fire at enemies that threaten the patrol boat – either warning shots or real shoot-to-kill.

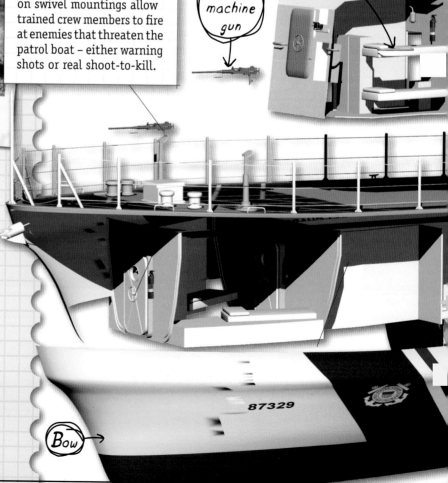

Berths (bunk beds)

M2 machine gun

Bow

87329

✳ For those in PERIL

Most national coastguards do SAR – search and rescue. They respond to emergency calls from stricken vessels that have run aground or lost engine power. Or perhaps a person has been swept overboard. In these cases the coastguard may have its own aircraft and helicopters to help, or perhaps it calls on the local air force, as it coordinates with the lifeboat service. Some nations limit their coastguards to SAR and watch-only patrols. If a patrol spots something suspicious, such as possible terrorists trying to land, at once they contact a branch of the military, usually the navy.

Watch a video of a patrol boat in action by visiting
www.factsforprojects.com and clicking on the web link.

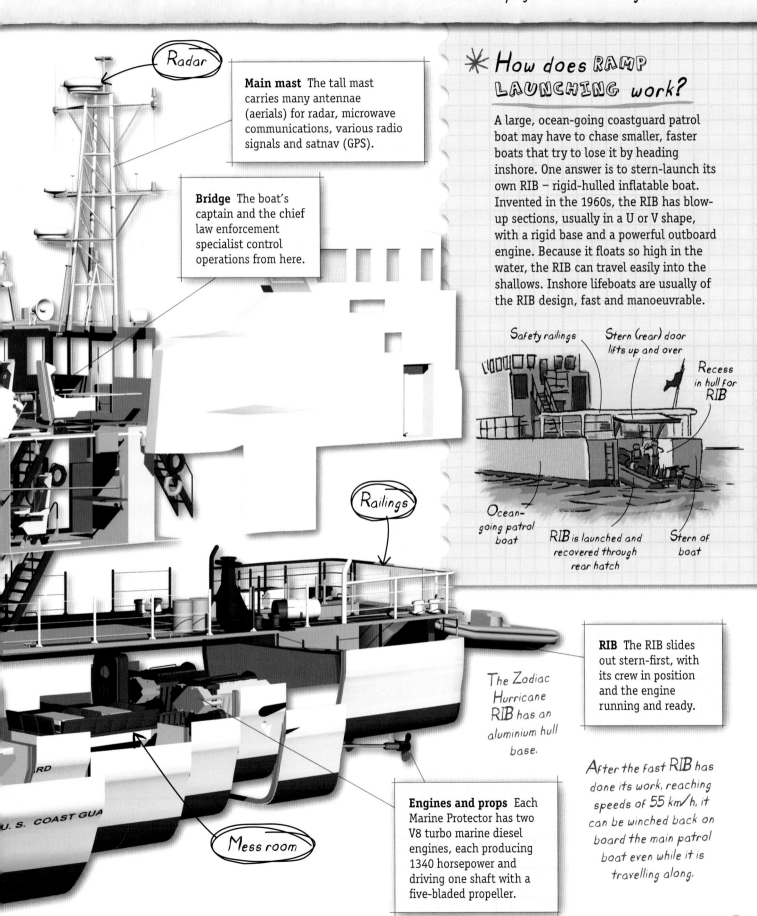

Radar

Main mast The tall mast carries many antennae (aerials) for radar, microwave communications, various radio signals and satnav (GPS).

Bridge The boat's captain and the chief law enforcement specialist control operations from here.

Railings

Mess room

✳ How does RAMP LAUNCHING work?

A large, ocean-going coastguard patrol boat may have to chase smaller, faster boats that try to lose it by heading inshore. One answer is to stern-launch its own RIB – rigid-hulled inflatable boat. Invented in the 1960s, the RIB has blow-up sections, usually in a U or V shape, with a rigid base and a powerful outboard engine. Because it floats so high in the water, the RIB can travel easily into the shallows. Inshore lifeboats are usually of the RIB design, fast and manoeuvrable.

Safety railings

Stern (rear) door lifts up and over

Recess in hull for RIB

Ocean-going patrol boat

RIB is launched and recovered through rear hatch

Stern of boat

RIB The RIB slides out stern-first, with its crew in position and the engine running and ready.

The Zodiac Hurricane RIB has an aluminium hull base.

Engines and props Each Marine Protector has two V8 turbo marine diesel engines, each producing 1340 horsepower and driving one shaft with a five-bladed propeller.

After the fast RIB has done its work, reaching speeds of 55 km/h, it can be winched back on board the main patrol boat even while it is travelling along.

U.S. COAST GUA

UNDERWATER RESCUE SUBMERSIBLE

Rescue missions are dangerous enough, but when they are in deep water, the risks multiply. The enormous water pressure brings great hazards since it crushes anything not built to withstand its huge pressing force – including human lungs. Most underwater rescue sites are also very cold and dark. And there is a time limit as the air supply runs lower and lower.

Eureka!

A forerunner of the rescue sub, the diving bell is a bell-shaped chamber lowered into water, trapping air inside. Divers can enter it for a few breaths. In use for more than 2000 years, the 16th century saw greatly improved versions.

Whatever next?

Personal survival suits are common for people exposed to risk at the water's surface. Underwater pressurized versions have been tested to depths of 100 metres.

The world record dive for crewed submersibles is 10,911 m, set in 1960 by Trieste.

The LR5 submersible rescue vessel has a maximum working depth of about 400 m.

Safety cage A metal cage surrounds the front windows to protect against rocks and other objects.

Pressure dome windows A spherical or domed shape is very good at resisting pressure, spreading out the force evently. So curved surfaces are used wherever possible for the sub's design.

A rescue sub being prepared for transportation

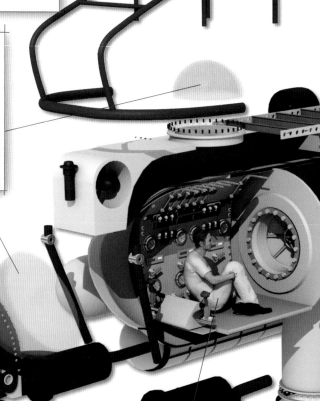

✳ To the RESCUE

The rescue submersible is a very specialized vessel, designed for careful manoeuvring at slow speeds. It cannot get to a rescue site under its own power, so it is transported by various means, as quickly as possible. Methods include a low-loader truck, a flatbed railway wagon, or even a cargo aircraft, and then the final stage by a 'mother ship' to the surface above the rescue site. The mother ship stays in position, or on station, ready to receive the rescued people who may need medical care.

Remote arm A manipulator arm can grab, move and cut objects such as cables, rocks or weeds. There is also a powerful cutting or grinding disc.

The LR5 is 9.2 m long and 3 m wide, with a hull height of 2.75 m.

Crew The standard crew of three is pilot, co-pilot and systems officer. They can be joined by up to 16 people at 'cram capacity' in the rescue chamber.

Rescue hatch

The LR5 travels at only 4 km/h, but it can position itself very precisely.

Discover more information and see images of the LR5 submersible by visiting www.factsforprojects.com and clicking on the web link.

Before it has to recharge its batteries, the LR5 can carry out up to eight diving missions.

LR5 SUBMERSIBLE

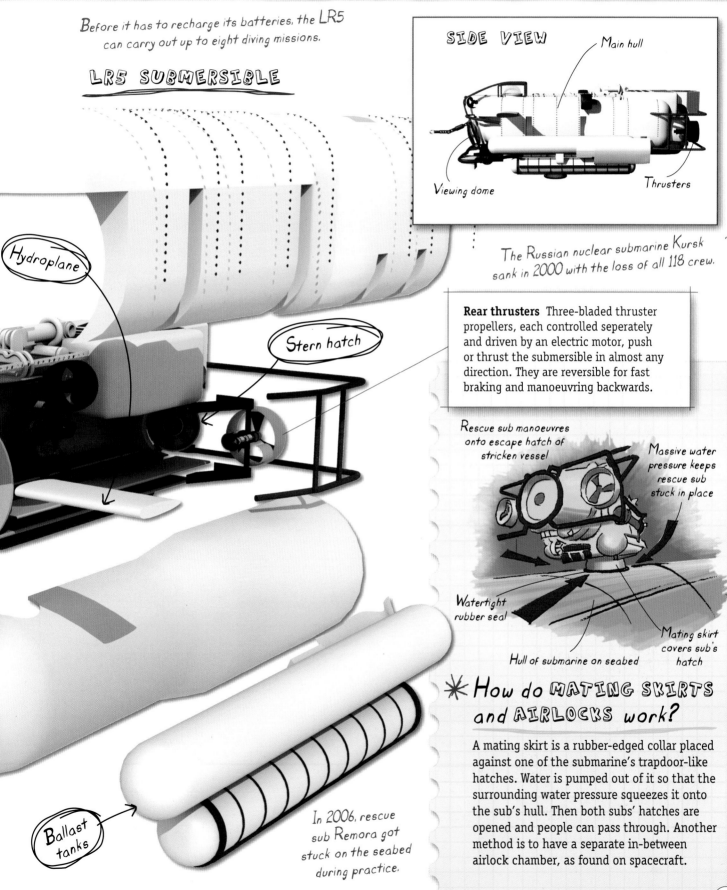

SIDE VIEW

Main hull

Viewing dome

Thrusters

Hydroplane

Stern hatch

The Russian nuclear submarine Kursk sank in 2000 with the loss of all 118 crew.

Rear thrusters Three-bladed thruster propellers, each controlled seperately and driven by an electric motor, push or thrust the submersible in almost any direction. They are reversible for fast braking and manoeuvring backwards.

Rescue sub manoeuvres onto escape hatch of stricken vessel

Massive water pressure keeps rescue sub stuck in place

Watertight rubber seal

Mating skirt covers sub's hatch

Hull of submarine on seabed

Ballast tanks

In 2006, rescue sub Remora got stuck on the seabed during practice.

✳ How do MATING SKIRTS and AIRLOCKS work?

A mating skirt is a rubber-edged collar placed against one of the submarine's trapdoor-like hatches. Water is pumped out of it so that the surrounding water pressure squeezes it onto the sub's hull. Then both subs' hatches are opened and people can pass through. Another method is to have a separate in-between airlock chamber, as found on spacecraft.

AIR AMBULANCE HELICOPTER

Blocked roads, flooded fields and broken bridges are no barriers to the air ambulance – a helicopter with life-saving equipment and a doctor or other trained medical staff. All it needs is a small patch of ground, such as a cleared roadway or farmer's field, for landing. Air ambulances also rush critical patients from one hospital to another more specialized centre, and carry donated body parts such as kidneys or hearts.

Eureka!

The first 'flying doctor' organization was set up in Australia in the 1920s. It was the brainchild of religious minister and keen pilot John Flynn (1880–1951). It used aircraft to take sick people to the nearest hospital, which could be hundreds of kilometres away.

Whatever next?

Helicopters are excellent at vertical take-off and landing, but forward speed is relatively slow. Tilt-wing aircraft, where wings and engines swivel through 90°, may take over.

Crew The highly trained pilot may be joined by a co-pilot or a helicopter-based paramedic, depending on the flying distance and conditions.

✳ How is a HELICOPTER controlled?

Flying a helicopter is different to flying an ordinary aircraft. The helicopter pilot has three sets of controls. The rudder foot pedals control yaw, or swivelling around left and right. The collective lever, which looks like a car handbrake, controls the rate of climb – going up or down – and also has the engine speed throttle. The cyclic lever, positioned like a plane's control column or 'joystick', adjusts the flight direction – forwards, back or sideways.

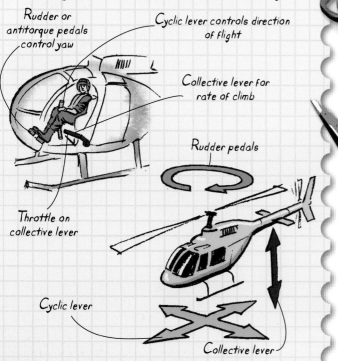

Rudder or antitorque pedals control yaw

Cyclic lever controls direction of flight

Collective lever for rate of climb

Rudder pedals

Throttle on collective lever

Cyclic lever

Collective lever

Emergency supplies First aid equipment includes drugs and medicines, oxygen masks, splints and bandages, and a defibrillator to restart a heart that has stopped or is fibrillating (beating with an abnormal rate and rhythm).

Stretcher The patient usually lies on the stretcher, strapped down in case of turbulence, where the medical staff can give mid-air care.

To see the crew of an air ambulance in action go to www.factsforprojects.com and click on the web link.

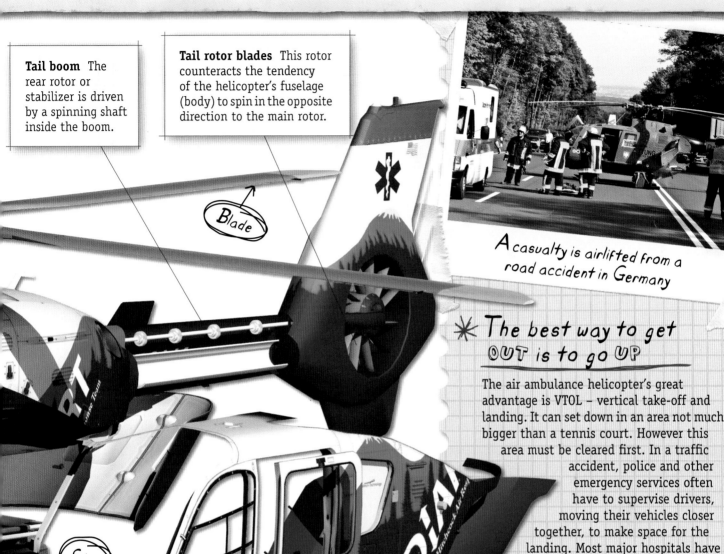

A casualty is airlifted from a road accident in Germany

Tail boom The rear rotor or stabilizer is driven by a spinning shaft inside the boom.

Tail rotor blades This rotor counteracts the tendency of the helicopter's fuselage (body) to spin in the opposite direction to the main rotor.

Blade

Step

Sliding windows

DartMouth-H^ck Medical Cente

✳ The best way to get OUT is to go UP

The air ambulance helicopter's great advantage is VTOL – vertical take-off and landing. It can set down in an area not much bigger than a tennis court. However this area must be cleared first. In a traffic accident, police and other emergency services often have to supervise drivers, moving their vehicles closer together, to make space for the landing. Most major hospitals have a dedicated landing site or helipad, which is always kept free.

Left door The large doors must allow stretchers and big pieces of medical equipment to pass through. Equipment may include a portable X-ray machine to check the patient for broken bones or fractures. The medical staff then radio ahead the patient's condition to specialists at the waiting hospital.

In some countries an air ambulance does other jobs when not needed for emergencies, such as checking electricity power lines or pipelines.

Landing skids Skids offer the best all-round landing ability. They are less likely to sink into soft ground than wheels and can cope with an uneven surface such as a ploughed field.

Treating a patient in mid air is very different from on the ground. A bumpy flight means that delicate procedures such as putting a needle into a vein become more difficult. Also the medic cannot hear the patient's heartbeat or breathing sounds due to the helicopter's noise.

SAR HELICOPTER

Search and rescue, SAR, saves thousands of lives daily around the world. Its workhorses are helicopters or 'choppers', usually air force types modified for rescue work. For people stranded up mountains, on cliffs, in remote canyons, in quicksand or out at sea, and perhaps injured too, the 'chop-chop-chop' of rotating blades means help has arrived. For rough-weather rescue, pilots need to be the best.

Eureka!

The first helicopter hoist rescue was in 1945. Two men were lifted by a Sikorsky R-5 from a stranded oil barge near Fairfield, Connecticut, USA. The violent storm meant no other method was possible.

Whatever next?

Helicopters continue to improve their performance, especially in high winds, when new electronic aids and advanced computer programs help the pilot.

Drive shaft

Radome

✳ Hold it STEADY!

High winds and crashing waves demand the highest piloting skills. One of the many difficulties is downdraft, where the downwards rush of air from the rotors causes spray, waves and wind at the water's surface. This can soak, blow sideways or even capsize (tip over) small vessels such as rowing boats. The pilot must hover high enough to minimize this problem. But greater height means a greater length of hoist cable, which makes it less controllable as it sways or swings in the downdraft and wind.

NAVY RESCUE
HS-12

Winch A powerful electric winch lowers and raises a hook, harness or other attachment on a long steel cable. The winch operator trains closely with the pilot.

The SAR version of the Sea King has a top speed of 267 km/h and a total range of 1000 km.

Rescue crew The winchman (winchperson) uses a combination of hand signals and spoken radio messages to communicate with the winch operator and pilot, to be placed onto the right spot and then winched up when all is ready.

A chopper lifts a casualty from a lifeboat, for the dash to hospital

Play a search and rescue game by visiting
www.factsforprojects.com and clicking on the web link.

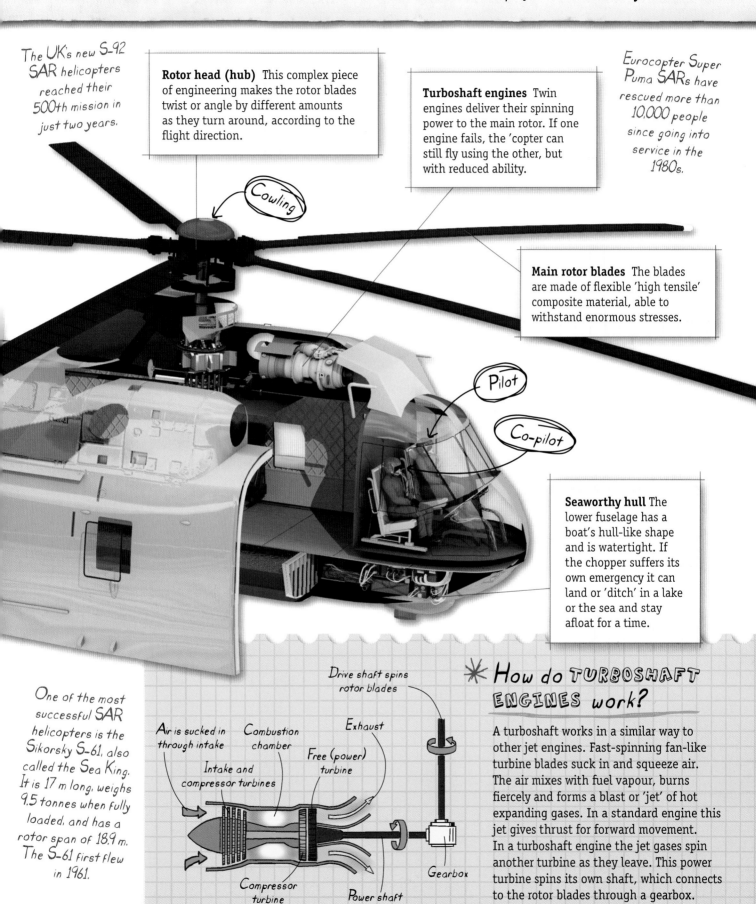

The UK's new S-92 SAR helicopters reached their 500th mission in just two years.

Rotor head (hub) This complex piece of engineering makes the rotor blades twist or angle by different amounts as they turn around, according to the flight direction.

Cowling

Turboshaft engines Twin engines deliver their spinning power to the main rotor. If one engine fails, the 'copter can still fly using the other, but with reduced ability.

Eurocopter Super Puma SARs have rescued more than 10,000 people since going into service in the 1980s.

Main rotor blades The blades are made of flexible 'high tensile' composite material, able to withstand enormous stresses.

Pilot

Co-pilot

Seaworthy hull The lower fuselage has a boat's hull-like shape and is watertight. If the chopper suffers its own emergency it can land or 'ditch' in a lake or the sea and stay afloat for a time.

One of the most successful SAR helicopters is the Sikorsky S-61, also called the Sea King. It is 17 m long, weighs 9.5 tonnes when fully loaded, and has a rotor span of 18.9 m. The S-61 first flew in 1961.

Air is sucked in through intake

Combustion chamber

Intake and compressor turbines

Drive shaft spins rotor blades

Exhaust

Free (power) turbine

Gearbox

Compressor turbine

Power shaft

✳ How do TURBOSHAFT ENGINES work?

A turboshaft works in a similar way to other jet engines. Fast-spinning fan-like turbine blades suck in and squeeze air. The air mixes with fuel vapour, burns fiercely and forms a blast or 'jet' of hot expanding gases. In a standard engine this jet gives thrust for forward movement. In a turboshaft engine the jet gases spin another turbine as they leave. This power turbine spins its own shaft, which connects to the rotor blades through a gearbox.

GLOSSARY

Alloy

A combination of metals, or metals and other substances, for special purposes such as great strength, extreme lightness, resistance to high temperatures, or all of these.

Ballast

A heavy substance, such as water, concrete or metal, added to a craft or vehicle to make it more stable and to stop it toppling over, for example, in high winds or when turning at speed. Many boats and ships have ballast tanks low in the hull that can be flooded with water if the vessel is not fully loaded. This allows them to float at the correct level and remain steady while moving and turning.

Bearing

A part designed for efficient movement, to reduce friction and wear, for example, between a spinning shaft or axle and its frame.

Blade

In aircraft, one of the long, slim parts of a propeller (airscrew) or helicopter rotor. Some propellers have six blades or more.

Boom

A long, slim, arm-like part of a crane or similar machine that can usually move up and down, from side to side and perhaps in and out.

Bow

In watercraft, the forward-pointing part of the hull (main body).

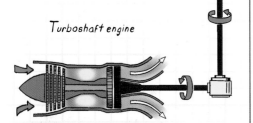

Turboshaft engine

Bridge

In watercraft, the control room of a large boat or ship, housing the wheel (steering wheel), engine throttles, instrument displays and other important equipment.

Bulkhead

An upright wall or partition across the width of a structure, such as across the hull of a ship or the fuselage of an aircraft.

Chassis

The main structural framework or 'skeleton' of a car, that gives it strength, and to which other parts are fixed, like the engine and seats.

Combustion chamber

A chamber where fuel combusts (burns) to produce high-pressure gases, as in a rocket engine.

Cylinder

In an engine or mechanical part, the chamber inside which a well-fitting piston moves.

Diesel engine

An internal combustion engine (one that burns or combusts fuel inside a chamber, the cylinder) that uses diesel fuel, and causes this to explode by pressure alone rather than by a spark plug.

Disc brake

A braking system where two stationary pads or pistons press onto either side of a rotating flat disc attached to the wheel, to slow it down.

Drive shaft

A spinning shaft from an engine or motor that drives or powers another part, such as the propeller of a water vessel.

Ramp launching

Fuselage

The main body or central part of an aircraft, usually long and tube-shaped.

Gears

Toothed wheels or sprockets that fit or mesh together so that one turns the other. If they are connected by a chain or belt with holes where the teeth fit, they are generally called sprockets. Gears are used to change turning speed and force, for example, between an engine and the road wheels of a car, or to change the direction of rotation.

GPS

Global Positioning System, a network of more than 20 satellites in space going around the Earth. They send out radio signals about their position and the time, allowing people to find their location using GPS receivers or 'satnavs'.

Hull

The main body or central part of a water vessel, and also of some land vehicles such as tanks.

Hydraulic

Machinery that works by using high-pressure liquid such as oil or water.

Infra-red

A form of energy, as rays or waves, which is similar to light but with longer waves that have a warming or heating effect.

Mast

On a watercraft, an upright or almost upright pole or spar that holds up and supports various items such as sails, flags and radar and radio equipment.

Petrol engine

An internal combustion engine (one that burns or combusts fuel inside a chamber, the cylinder) that uses petrol fuel and causes this to explode using a spark plug.

Piston

A wide, rod-shaped part, similar in shape to a food or drinks can, that moves along or up and down inside a close-fitting chamber, the cylinder.

Pneumatic

Machinery that works by high-pressure gas such as air or oxygen.

Propeller

A spinning device with angled blades, like a rotating fan, that turns to draw in a fluid such as water or air at the front, and thrust it powerfully rearwards. Also called a waterscrew in water vessels or an airscrew in aircraft.

Radar

A system that sends out radio waves that reflect off objects such as aircraft or ships, and detects echoes to find out their position.

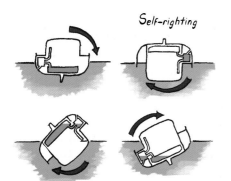

Self-righting

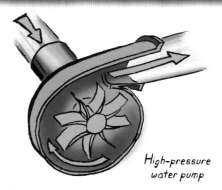

High-pressure water pump

Radiator

In cars and similar vehicles, a part designed to lose heat, for example, from an engine. It has a large surface area, usually lots of fins or vanes. Hot water from the engine circulates through it, to become cooler before flowing back to the engine.

Radio signals

Messages sent by invisible waves of combined electricity and magnetism, where each wave is quite long, from a few millimetres to many kilometres. (Light waves are similar but much shorter.)

Rudder

The control surface of an aircraft or watercraft, usually on the upright fin or 'tail' of an aircraft or below the rear hull of a boat, that makes it steer left or right (yaw).

Satellite

Any object that goes around or orbits another. For example, the Moon is a natural satellite of the Earth. The term is used especially for artificial or man-made orbiting objects, particularly those going around the Earth.

Satnav

Satellite navigation, finding your way and location using radio signals from the GPS (Global Positioning System) satellites in space.

Stern

In watercraft, the rear or blunt end of the hull.

Suspension

Parts that allow the road wheels or tracks of a vehicle to move up and down separately from the driver and passengers, to smooth out bumps and dips in the road. Also any similar system that gives a softer, more comfortable ride.

Throttle

A control that allows more fuel and air into the engine for greater speed, sometimes called an accelerator.

Thruster

A small propeller, nozzle or jet-like part that produces a pushing force, usually to make small adjustments to the position or direction of travel of a craft or vehicle.

Transmission

All the parts that transmit the turning force from the engine (crankshaft) to the wheel axles, including the gears, gearbox and propeller shaft.

Turbine

A set of angled fan-like blades on a spinning shaft, used in many areas of engineering, from pumps and cars to jet engines.

Turboshaft

A jet engine with fan-like turbine blades inside, which spins a shaft for power rather than using its jet blast of gases.

Puncture nozzle

INDEX